MW01486963

21 MORE Songs in 6 Days:

Learn Intermediate Ukulele the Easy Way

Rebecca Bogart & Jenny Peters

Contents

Why You Should Buy This Book

Learn New Skills and Chords

In *21 Songs in 6 Days: Learn Intermediate Ukulele the Easy Way* we presented the five most common ukulele chords (C, F, A Minor, C7 and G7) and the three basic strums that are the building blocks of intermediate and advanced ukulele. This book picks up where the previous one left off.

You'll learn some great new skills in this book:

- How to play 10 new chords.

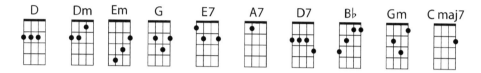

- How to combine the three basic strums you already know into more complicated patterns
- How to play melodies on your ukulele. This style of playing is called "fingerpicking melodies."
- How to play chords in a new style where you pluck one string at a time. This style is called "fingerpicking accompaniment" or "fingerpicking broken chords."
- How to play melodies and chords at the same time on your ukulele. This style of playing is called "solo ukulele" or "chord melody" playing.

Learn 21 MORE Songs

Just like in *21 Songs in 6 Days,* we'll learn these skills by playing songs, not boring exercises.

- Twinkle, Twinkle Little Star
- Taps
- Shave and a Haircut
- Amazing Grace (Melody)
- Lonely Blues
- New Chord Blues
- Lazy Sailor
- On Top of Old Smokey
- Bicycle Built for Two
- Wayfaring Stranger
- The Erie Canal
- Scarborough Fair
- The House of the Rising Sun
- Swing Low, Sweet Chariot
- Michael, Row the Boat Ashore
- Oh Susanna
- Won't You Come Home Bill Bailey
- You Are My Sunshine

- Oh When the Saints (Solo Ukulele Version)
- Amazing Grace (Solo Ukulele Version)
- Aura Lee (Solo Ukulele Version)
- Aloha Oe (Solo Ukulele Version)

Speaking of *21 Songs in 6 Days*, if you have any difficulty with the material in this book, you can get all the basics under your belt by working through its 6 days and 40+ lesson videos. Get your copy.at ukulele.io/Buy21Songs

Lots of Ways to Play Each Song

We usually suggest several strumming patterns for each song. The easier patterns are great when you are first learning a song. Upgrade to a more difficult pattern as you gain skill.

All of the songs are written out on a standard music *staff* with a *treble clef*. Lyrics appear below the staff, and a chord letter appears above each time there's a chord change. Readers who prefer to play their uke by ear will find that the lyrics and chord changes are all they need. Those who like to read music will find everything they need to play new songs in no time.

We've also included ukulele *tablature* notation for all 21 songs in this book. The *tab staff* works like a road map showing you how to pluck the melody on the strings of the ukulele. This way you can either sing the song and strum the chords, or play the melody on your uke. If you have a friend or family member who plays ukulele, you can create duets, with one person playing melody and the other one strumming chords.

If you don't recognize any of the musical terms shown in *bold italic letters*, just turn to the glossary on page 97, where you'll find an alphabetical list of them for easy reference. There's also a chord glossary with photos and chord stamps for each chord used in this book.

Harness the Power of Video Learning Online or by DVD

Each song has an accompanying online lesson video with lyrics and chord changes so you can hear as well as see the music. It's a very enjoyable way to learn musical skills. To set up your member account at our website, please follow the directions on page 8: "How to Sign Up for the Members' Area of ukulele.io ". If you're not really an online person, you can purchase a DVD of all the lessons in this book at ukulele.io/21MoreDVD.

With *21 MORE Songs in 6 Days: Learn Intermediate Ukulele the Easy Way* you'll be excited to pick up your ukulele and tackle new music!

Want Free Stuff?

Not ready to commit? Visit ukulele.io/freestuff to sign up for free lesson videos, tab sheet music for ukulele, and news about other uke books. To get all this free stuff, you need to give us your email address. We never sell or rent our email list, so you don't need to worry about spam or losing your privacy.

About this Book

Welcome to *21 MORE Songs in 6 Days: Learn Intermediate Ukulele the Easy Way!* We're glad you're here. A few details before we get started.

Words in **bold italics** are defined in the glossary at the end of the book.

Be sure to look at the section called "How to Sign Up for the Members' Area at ukulele.io" on page 8. You'll find instructions there about how to access the online lesson videos. Or you can purchase a DVD of all the lesson videos at ukulele.io/21MoreDVD.

In the lesson videos we perform a simple arrangement of each tune:
1. We sing and strum one or two verses
2. Jenny plays the melody and Rebecca strums the chords
3. We sing and strum another verse and/or chorus to round out the song.

Use your own imagination and preferences to come up with a way that works best for you.

Some Notes on Strumming

Here are the three basic strumming patterns we will refer to in this book.

Strum #1 All down strums on a steady ***beat***

Strum #2 Down-up strums with an even division of the beat. All the strums are equally spaced.

Strum #3 Down-up strums with an uneven division of the beat. Wait a little longer after each down strum before you play the next up strum.

Here's music notation showing the rhythm of Strum #3.

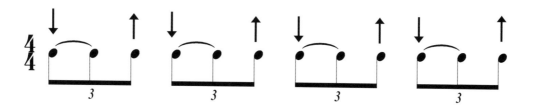

Use the fingernails of your right hand for the down strum and the thumbnail of your right hand for the up strum. Learning these patterns takes time. If your fingers get sore, don't worry. It can take a while to build up thicker skin.

We'll suggest some more complicated strums later in the book that are derived from these three basic patterns.

Thanks for buying this book. We hope you enjoy it along with the online lesson videos. Sharing is a good thing, so why not leave a review of *21 MORE Songs in 6 Days* on Amazon? Here's a convenient link: ukulele.io/21MOREreview. Your review will help other ukulele book shoppers make their decision about what to buy.

How to Sign Up for the Members' Area of ukulele.io

Before you go any farther, please visit the link below and sign up for the members-only area of ukulele.io. The special private link below is the ONLY way to get access to the video lessons for this book. You will only need to do this once. We'll send you an email with your user name and password so you won't forget them.

ukulele.io/21more

If you already have a ukulele.io account, you still need to visit this url to upgrade your member level to access the videos for this book.

Once you've created your account using the private link above, then you can access the members' area from the home page of ukulele.io. Simply click the red "login" button in the upper right corner to enter the members' area.

If you have any trouble creating an account, please drop us a note at ukulele.io/contact-us. We want you to start learning ukulele as quickly as possible!

Another option if you just don't want to deal with member accounts, logins, and websites is to purchase the video lessons on DVD. Get yours at ukulele.io/21MoreDVD.

Chapter 1 – Reading Melodies and Tab

Remember to visit ukulele.io/21more and sign up for the members' area at ukulele.io so you can use the free video lessons that come with this book.

In this chapter, we're going to show you a great shorthand system for learning melodies from a printed page or computer screen. In other words, you can learn to play a melody that you've never heard before by reading it the same way you are reading the words of this book.

Tablature, or tab for short, is the easiest way to read song melodies and learn to play them on your ukulele. It is a visual code that tells your left hand which fret to stop and your right hand which string to pluck. When your hands follow the code correctly, you will hear a recognizable melody coming out of your ukulele!

Tab is different from regular musical notation. We show both in all of our songs – the standard music notation is the top staff and the tab notation is the bottom staff. We present the songs this way because some folks might already know how to read regular music notation and find that it helps them read the tab. If you don't know how to read standard musical notation, just ignore the top staff.

We're going to start learning tab with *Are You Sleeping?* We're hoping you already know this melody so you can use your ear to help you judge whether you are following the tab notation correctly. Another reason we're starting with *Are You Sleeping?* is that it is easy to play - your left hand doesn't have to move at all to play this melody.

How to Read Tab Notation

Each line of the tab staff represents a string on the ukulele. Unfortunately, they're upside down from how they are arranged on the ukulele. So the top line of the tab staff is the A-string (the string closest to the floor when you're playing). The tab staff line below the top line is the E-string. The line below that is the C-string. The bottom line of the tab is the G-string, which is the string closest to the ceiling when you are playing.

The numbers on the lines tell you which *fret* to play. A 0 means to *pluck* a string with your right hand without using your left hand at all. A 1 means to put one of your left hand fingers in the first fret and push down on the string. This is called "*fretting*" or "*stopping*" the string. A 2 means to stop the string in the second fret. The numbers can go as high as 19 because the ukulele has 19 frets, but we have never seen notation for anything higher in pitch than 12.

Here's an excerpt from *This Land Is Your Land.* To read the tab, first look at which string line the number is on. Then use your left hand to stop that string in the fret that matches the number shown. Remember that 0 means an open string. We've labeled the lines to make it easier to see which line goes with which string.

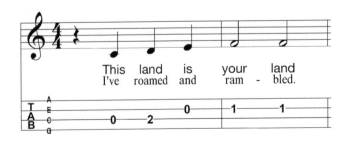

- For the first note, don't do anything with your left hand and pluck the C-string with your right hand.

- For the second note, stop the C-string in the 2nd fret with your left hand and pluck it with your right hand.

- For the third note, don't do anything with your left hand and pluck the E-string with your right hand.

- Continue through the song using your ear to help you learn how tab works.

We've made a lesson video with a special onscreen format to help you learn tab. As you watch the video lesson, you'll hear the way the music should sound. You'll also see lots of visual cues to help you link how the tab looks with how the music sounds.

The tab symbol that corresponds to the note you are hearing is circled in red in the video lesson. You'll see Jenny fretting and plucking the string in the main frame of the video and there's also a dot on the fretboard at the right of the screen to help you see which string and fret go with the tab symbol.

Remember, you can access the video lessons by visiting ukulele.io/21more to set up your member account.

Fingerpicking Technique

Here's how to use your hands two different ways to fingerpick the melodies of the songs.

- Plucking with your index finger: use this method for a faster song. Put your right thumb against the edge of the fretboard and pluck with your right index finger, pulling the string toward the ceiling to make the sound. This method will give you more rhythmic control and let you play faster.

- Plucking with your thumb: use this method for a slower song. This method will give you a richer sound.

As you work your way through this book, we'll also teach you how to fingerpick chords one note at a time (called "broken" chords) and how to do techniques like the "hammer on" and "pull off" for quickly moving melody notes.

Three Melodies to Learn Tab

We'll be using three melodies to learn how to fingerpick and read tab. They all stay in what we call *first position*. On a stringed instrument, the first position is when the first finger of your left hand is in the first fret. Because none of the frets are higher than 3 you can play the whole song without moving your left hand. It's easiest to begin with melodies where your left hand can stay put so you can concentrate on learning to pluck with your right hand and getting your brain and eyes to understand tab notation.

We chose *Are You Sleeping?* for our first song because it has one of the most familiar melodies in the world. At the end of the song, the melody you play on your ukulele will sound different than how you would sing it because it will go up, rather than down. We've written the melody this way because unless you have a ukulele with "low G" tuning, C is the lowest note you can play. This kind of change is called an *octave transposition*.

Twinkle, Twinkle Little Star is next. It's familiar and it uses lots of open strings. We like that! But it is a little more complicated than *Are You Sleeping?* because you have to skip over frets and change strings with your both left and right hands as you play the melody. .

The third melody, *Oh When the Saints,* is a little faster than *Twinkle.*

Tips to Practice Smart

Look for Repeated Patterns

When you first begin to learn a song from printed tab or music notation, it is a good idea to look through the whole song and see where there are parts that are the same, and where there are parts that are different. The lyrics can also help you see where there is repetition in the song.

Oh When the Saints, like most songs, has a lot of small sections that are repeated. Notice how the first line repeats the same pattern of music notes and tablature symbols. The beginning of the second line also uses the same repeating pattern. But the last two lines are very different from the first two lines.

Practice in Small Chunks

The most efficient way to practice any song is to learn it as a series of smaller chunks. The ear, brain and fingers are able to retain patterns much more easily when we repeat small sections (5-8 bits of information or notes) than when we repeat longer patterns (i.e., the whole song).

Do the Hard Part More

Try to figure out which sections will be the most difficult and practice those the most. Usually if there are more or higher numbers on the tab staff, or more black notes on the music staff, the notes will move faster and/or be harder to play.

Learn to Start in the Middle

Resist the temptation to always go back to the beginning when you make a mistake! This technique will only make you very good at playing the beginning (the easiest part of this song) at the expense of spending time on the part that is hard for you! It can feel difficult at first to start in the middle of a song, but the work you do to learn how to start in the middle will help imprint that section into your mind.

Practice Plan for Oh When the Saints

Here's a practice plan showing you how to apply our practice smart tips to learning *Oh When the Saints.* There is also a lesson video showing you how to apply this practice plan.

It's best to begin your practice sessions with the most difficult section because this will imprint it more firmly into your memory. So for this song it is best to begin with the fourth line because it is the most difficult. Play it several times until it is easy.

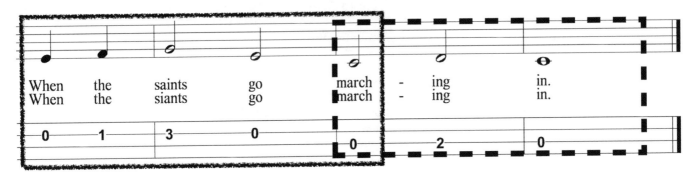

If you can't play it very well after two or three tries, then break it apart. Start with the sounds that go with the lyrics, "When the Saints Go March-." Then try playing the sounds that go with "Marching In." Then join all the sounds together so you have all of line four working well. Notice how the small practice sections overlap. The overlap makes it easy to put the sections back together without a pause.

Use the same approach with the third line. Play it several times until it is easy. If you can't play the whole line at once, break it apart. First play the four sounds that go with, "Oh Lord I want" three or four times. Then play the sounds that go with "want.....to be in that number" three or four times. Now connect the two parts together. Then repeat the third line until it is easy.

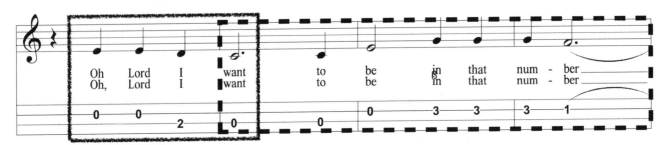

Next, learn the second line of tab. It should be a snap to learn this line because it is almost identical to the fourth line. The first line will need almost no practice now because it contains a pattern you already learned while practicing the second line. Now, it's finally time to start at the beginning and play to the end. Given the careful practicing you've done, the whole song should be easy now!

Our next song, *Shave and a Haircut,* is just a little snippet of music that's fun to add it at the end of songs. Musicians call this a "tag." This song is already so short that you probably won't need to break it into practice chunks.

The First Position and Beyond

When the first finger of your left hand stays in the first fret, you are playing in the first position. When you shift your hand down the fretboard, the name of the position changes to match the fret number where your first finger rests. For example, if the first finger of your left is resting on the third fret, you are playing in the third position.

Here are pictures of the left hand in the first and second positions on the ukulele fretboard.

First Position

Second Position

Third Position

Let's use the song *Taps* to learn the third position for your left hand on the ukulele fretboard. *Taps* is usually played by a bugler as the sun goes down to offer thanks for a good day. It's also played at military funerals. One of our relatives is a trumpeter and a military veteran. He volunteers to travel 50 miles or more to play this beautiful song at a veteran's funeral to bring the family comfort in a time of sadness.

Taps requires moving your hand up and down the fretboard, so we've added fingering numbers to the sheet music: they are the little numbers above the notes on the music staff. Move your first finger to the third fret, where your third finger usually goes. This is third position. Rest your 2nd finger in fret 5 and use your 4th finger to play fret 7. This way it will be easier to reach up to fret 7 and fret 10 as you need to go higher in the song.

We call this kind of open hand positon an extension because you spread four fingers to cover five frets. It's easiest to open between the first and second fingers of the left hand, because these are your strongest and most coordinated fingers. The extension technique prepares you to play the melody of *Amazing Grace*. If *Amazing Grace* seems too difficult to learn now, skip it. We will be studying it again later in the book to learn other techniques.

Extended Position for Amazing Grace

When it is time to play fret 10, you will need to shift your hand down the neck of the ukulele. Many ukuleles have a dot on fret 7 and fret 10 to help you find them. Handy! *Taps* is usually played slowly, so you can use the time between the notes to find the frets with your left hand.

Here are pictures of the left hand in the third, fourth and fifth position on the ukulele fretboard. If you find these pictures confusing, try turning the book upside down. This upside down view is what you see when you look down at your hand as you are holding your ukulele.

Third Position

Fourth Position

Fifth Position

Putting It All Together

Wow! You've learned how to play melodies on your ukulele. From now on, the rest of the songs in this book will be presented with melody line, tab line, chord shapes and a suggested strumming pattern.

Now that you know how to read tab, here are some great ways you can use your new knowledge.

- Sometimes it is fun to go back and forth picking out melodies and then returning to strumming chords.

- By the end of this book we want you to be familiar enough with melodies and chord shapes so that you can put it all together and play both at the same time. This is called "solo ukulele" or chord melody playing.

Are You Sleeping

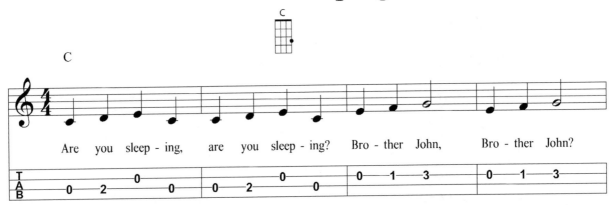

Twinkle, Twinkle Little Star

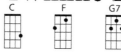

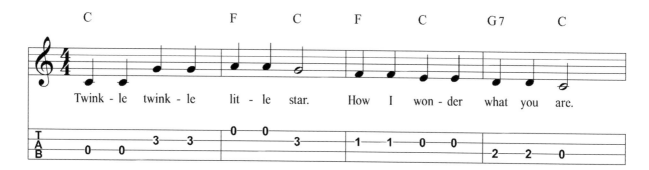

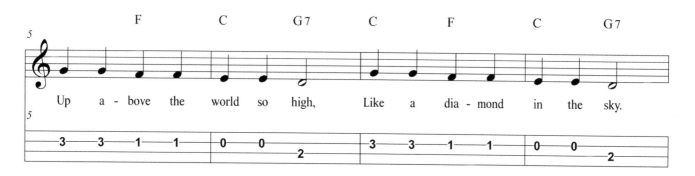

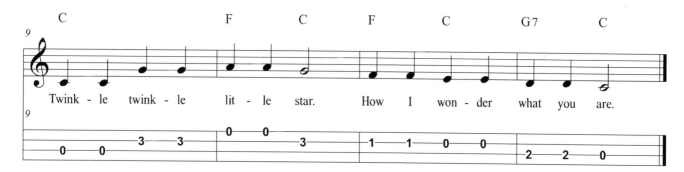

Oh When The Saints

Shave and a Haircut

Taps

Amazing Grace

Chapter 2 – Learning the 12 Bar Blues

Playing the blues is very satisfying since you can create a lot of great sounding music with just a few chords and strums. Learning blues basics gives you an opportunity to make up your own music because the blues is based on *improvisation*. Finally, the blues are easy and fun to play with someone else. You'll learn two blues songs in this chapter: *New Chord Blues* and *Lonely Blues*.

Blues is a uniquely American style of music that originated in the African American communities of the southern U.S. around the turn of the century. Many elements of the blues can be traced back to the music of Africa. It is a music associated with the freedom of former slaves. Most American popular music grew out of the blues. The first rock songs *(Johnny B. Goode, Rock Around the Clock, Ain't Nothin' But a Hound Dog)* all followed the 12 bar blues *chord progression*.

The Blues Progression

The blues uses a 12 measure chord progression consisting of three chords that have a specific pitch spacing and relationship to one another. ("Bar" is another word for "*measure*.") You already know the three chords to play these songs in the *scale* (also called "*key*") of C major: C, F, and G7. To help you remember them, we repeat the chord symbols and pictures of the chord shapes below.

C

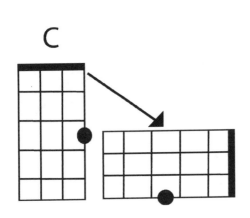

F

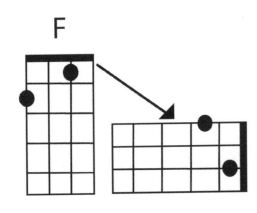

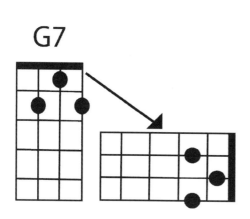

The official music theory names of these three chords are *tonic*, *subdominant* and *dominant*. The names refer to how each chord functions in a specific *scale* or *key*.

To understand that last abstract sentence, you might think of the words father, mother, daughter, brother. These nouns describe how people function or relate to one another within a family. So the tonic, dominant, and subdominant are like the father, mother, and daughter, and the "key" or "scale" is like a family – it is a group of sounds that are related to each other. (We'll explain a lot more about the relationships between scales and chords in Chapter 3.)

Musicians often refer to the tonic chord as the "one" chord, shown with the capital "I" symbol. The subdominant is referred to as the "four" chord, shown with the symbol IV, the Roman numeral for four.

The dominant is referred to as the "five" chord, shown with the symbol V or V7. If you see a chord symbol with one letter and the number 7 it is always a dominant 7th chord. The dominant 7th chords in this book are C7, G7, D7, A7, E7.

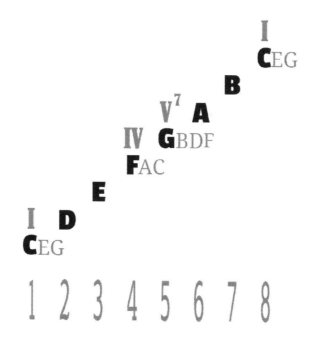

The simplest form of 12-bar blues uses the ***chord progression*** below. Each letter stands for a measure of music.

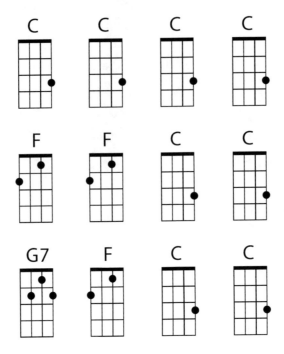

When you are first learning the pattern, strum four down strums for each chord symbol. When you are more comfortable, you can strum the pattern with Strum #3, the uneven down-up strumming pattern.

From Progression to Song

Blues songs are usually structured like a sandwich: someone sings, then someone plays melodies on an instrument, then someone sings again. In blues songs the 12 measure melody is usually repeated several times with different words.

Blues lyrics often tell stories of sadness. Usually, the first four measures of a blues song state a problem: "If your house catches fire and there ain't no water 'round". The next four repeat the problem, or restate it in stronger language. The final four measures offer a solution: "Throw your rags out the window, let the doggone shack burn down."

Next comes an instrumental section where a soloist improvises over the same chord progression that backed up the singer's melody. The song will often close with the singer repeating one of the original verses.

Blues Improvisation

Musical improvisation means to make up music as you are playing. Songs that use the 12-bar blues often have a section where one musician makes up new melodies while others continue to play the 12-bar blues progression. Blues melodies are always made from a specific family of notes called the blues scale. That's what makes them sound "bluesy."

To begin learning to improvise, we will first learn the Blues Scale. The music below shows two examples of the blues scale.

Blues Scale

Scale #1:

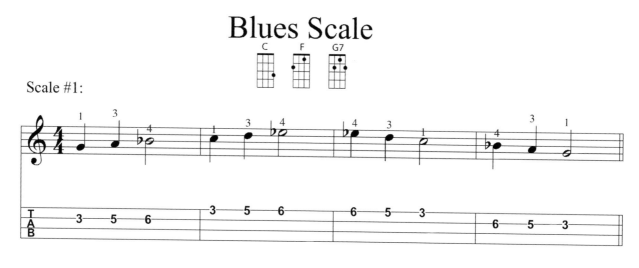

Scale #2:

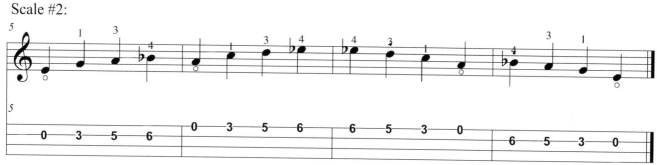

There are two staves of music: one of them is standard music notation and the other one is tablature. Please refer to page 10 for instructions on how to read the tab staff.

Here are some detailed instructions on how to play this music

- Pluck the single notes with your right thumb to get a ringing sound. You can also pluck with your long fingers if you prefer the sound, or if it is more comfortable for you.

- Move your left hand down the fretboard, so that your finger 1 (index finger) is in the third fret. We call this playing in the third position. (Refer to the photo on page 16)

- The numbers very near the music notes represent which left hand fingers to use to stop the strings. To play the first three notes, you would use fingers 1, then 3, then 4 to stop the 2nd string with your left hand in the third position. For the next three notes, use the same left hand fingers in the same order on the first string. For the next group of three notes, use fingers 1, 3, and 4 but in the reverse order: 4, then 3, then 1. And so on.

- Please be sure to watch the "Blues Scale" lesson video at ukulele.io. Remember, to access the lesson videos, visit ukulele.io/21More and create your member account. Once you've got an account you can log in and go to the Chapter 2 page to watch the Blues Scale lesson video.

How to Improvise

There is no right or wrong way to improvise. You can play the notes of the blues scale in any order and in any rhythm. Feel free to experiment with anything that strikes your fancy. But if you feel uncertain of how to begin, here are some suggestions to prime the pump.

Pick a very small musical idea (3-4 notes) and repeat it 2 to 3 times. Then play something different, and finally return to your original idea. Structuring your improvisation this way makes it easier to get started because you only have to think of one simple idea. Then you can use it to generate a lot of music.

Here's how to apply this suggestion more specifically to the blues progression. Think of a short one- or two-measure bit of music and play it during measures 1 and 2 and 5 and 6 of the chorus. Don't play anything during measures 3 and 4, or 7 and 8. In measure 9, begin with your short idea again but then make up something a little different to close out the 12 bar chorus.

Many of the great classical composers used this technique. Think of the first movement of Beethoven's *Fifth Symphony* – the main idea has even been picked up and used for TV commercials! Also, music that is structured with repetition and variation often sounds better to the listener. In fact, the blues progression is set up with a lot of repetition of the C chord, with gradually increasing contrast (the F and G7 in bars 10 and 11), followed by a return to the original idea (the C chord).

Another variable you can play with in your improvisation is rhythm. You could build an improvisation out of one or two notes by playing them with a catchy rhythm.

Not sure how to come up with rhythms? Think of a phrase of words and then play notes of the blues scale to match. In other words, find the pattern of long and short and weak and strong sounds that matches the words you thought of and then play your ukulele sounds in the same pattern. Here's an example: "The moose…is on the loose…" with long, strong sounds on "moose" and "loose."

It's often easier and more fun to improvise with someone else. If you have a friend who plays ukulele, you can play the notes in blues scale while your friend strums the 12-bar blues chord pattern. What's great is that all of the blues scale notes sound good when you improvise over the 12-bar blues chord progression.

Blues Songs

The blues songs in this chapter are original songs by Jenny Peters, one of the authors of this book. The improvisations are written out. You could also make up your own improvised music in the middle of each song.

Your first blues song to learn is *New Chord Blues*. We will revisit this song in Chapter 4 when we start to learn new chords.

The second blues song is *Lonely Blues*. It uses the same chord progression as *New Chord Blues*, but has a different melody and words. Like many blues songs, it tells a story of love gone wrong.

New Chord Blues in C

Lonely Blues

Jenny Peters

Chapter 3 – Etudes and Learning New Chords

We're assuming that you already know the five easiest and most common ukulele chords shown below.

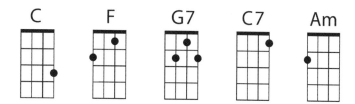

If not, we'll indulge in some shameless self promotion and suggest you purchase our first book, *21 Songs in 6 Days: Learn Intermediate Ukulele the Easy Way*. Get your copy at ukulele.io/Buy21Songs. But now, let's move on to some new slightly more difficult chords. We've chosen the 11 shown because they are the ones you will encounter most often as you venture into the world of ukulele clubs and online tabs and lessons.

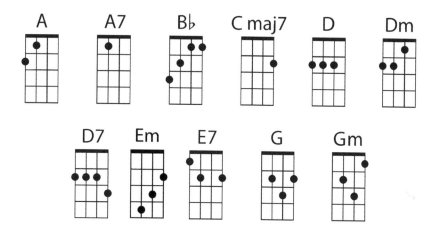

Don't expect to get these new chords all right away. If they are difficult, skip ahead to songs you like. You can always come back and to this chapter when these chords show up in music you are playing. We've put a Chord Glossary at the back of the book for easy reference. It contains chord symbols and photographs of how your hand should look when you are playing these chords.

Now, 11 chords is a lot to learn all at once, so we are going to break down the new chords into smaller, easier to digest groups.

Let's Go for Quality: Major, Minor and Dominant

Before we tell you about the groups, we'd like to teach you a little about types of chords. Each chord uses different notes, strings, and finger positions on the fretboard, but they can be grouped t based on how they sound. The official name of this way of typing chords by their sound is chord "quality."

First, you need to know that in basic (non-jazz) music there are three main chord qualities or types: Major, Minor and Dominant.

Major chords have just a letter for their name. Major chords sound happy and complete. Songs like *Happy*

Birthday and *Take Me Out to the Ball Game* have mostly major chords in them. The new Major chords in this book are

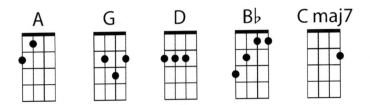

The first four of these chords are triads, which means there only 3 notes in each chord. The Cmaj7 is still a Major chord, but it has a fourth note (called the 7th) and makes an ear tickling progression with the C Major and C7 chords.

Minor chords have a capital letter followed by a lower case m (or sometimes min) to indicate minor. Minor chords sound stable and complete, but they give the listener a sense of sadness or darkness. Beethoven's *Fifth Symphony* or the song *Erie Canal* have a lot of minor chords. Minor chords are often added to a major key song to give it a more varied sound. The new minor chords in this book are:

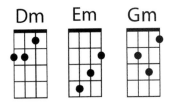

Dominant 7th chords are written with a capital letter followed by the number 7. These chords give the listener a sense of leading into another chord. If a song ends on a Dominant 7 chord, the song will feel unfinished. The new Dominant 7th chords are:

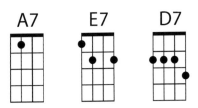

Chords Run in Packs

Out in the wild wild world of music, chords don't randomly mix up together. Certain chords are usually found near one another, and some chords show up much more then than others. That's because chords are related to each other in very specific ways. The study of how chords relate is called music theory or harmony, and it is a big and complicated subject. But here's what you, the ukulele learner, need to know in a nutshell.

Related chords, also known as chord families, are built from a specific set of *pitches* or *notes*, called a *scale*. Most Western music is built from major or minor scales which both have 8 notes. (In fact, minor scales use the same notes as major scales, just starting at a different point in the sequence.)

A major scale uses seven different notes or pitches; the eighth note is the same as the first one. We give the different sounds or pitches you can play on your ukulele by plucking one string a name. The sounds are named with the letters of the alphabet A through G.

Here are the names of the pitches of the C scale. These notes would all be white keys on the piano. We show them going up from left to right because that is how notes going up in pitch would be shown on a music staff.

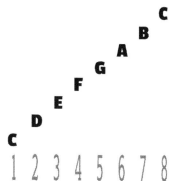

Why the fascination with C major? Because C major is one of the easiest scales to play on the ukulele, since the open strings of the ukulele count for 4 of the 8 scale notes. That's why many of the chords of C major can be made with only one or two fingers – you're able to use open strings for many of the notes of the chord.

Chords of C Major Scale

The chords of the C Major scale are made out of the same pitches as the scale of C Major. The main chords of every scale are built on scale notes numbers 1, 2, 3, 4, 5, 6. (There is also a chord built on scale note number 7 but it is not used very much so we are leaving it out for now).

Musicians sometimes describe where a chord lives inside its scale by using a Roman numeral. Major chords are shown with capital Roman numerals and minor chords are shown with lower case Roman numerals. So the chord family of the C Major scale is as follows.

I. C Major C E G. This chord is sometimes called the "tonic" chord.
ii. D Minor D F A
iii E Minor E G B
IV F Major F A C. This chord is sometimes called the "subdominant" chord.
V G Dominant 7th G B D F This chord is sometimes called the "dominant" chord.
Vi A Minor A C E

Notice how all the letters that make up the chords are the same as the letters that make up the scale. That's what we mean when we say that C F G and A minor are chords of the key or scale of C major. Also notice how the C Major chord family has some major chords, some minor chords, and one dominant 7th chord. Chord families built on major scales always have three major chords, 2 minor chords, and one dominant 7th per scale.

Here's a picture of the C scale triads. We've only shown the symbols for the most important chords, the I (tonic), IV (subdominant) and V7 (dominant). By important we mean the chords that are used the most often.

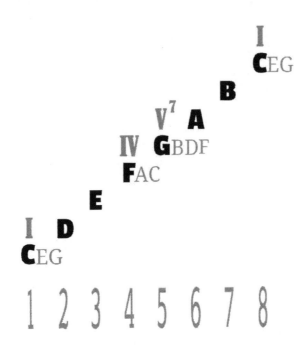

Phew. That was a lot of music theory. If you don't understand it after reading it, don't worry. As you play chord families and songs, you'll begin to hear and feel in your hands how certain chords often occur together. Frequently they show up in the same order over and over again. In fact, chords occur so often in the same order that musicians have a special name for specific sequences of chords: ***chord progression***.

We're going to organize our study of new chords by learning some chord progressions. Here are some important progressions to learn and practice. We will give you three ***etudes*** or studies to learn these new chords. Think of these etudes as running hills or doing weight lifting - something you know is worth the long term gain but maybe not so easy in the moment.

The Blues Progression

In Chapter 2 we learned the 12 bar blues progression. It uses the I, IV and V7 chords of a major scale. We learned it in the scale of C Major, so the chords were:

    I   CEG   C major chord
    IV FAC   F major chord
    V7 GBDF G dominant 7 chord.

In the next chapter we're going to learn the 12 bar blues progression in the scales of F, G, and D. Because the blues progression uses the most important chords of the major scale (I, IV, and V, or tonic, subdominant, and dominant) it's an efficient way to learn new chords.

Etude #1–The Descending C Scale with Chords

Here's an etude that has you playing almost all the chords of the C scale. It's hard work but you will learn a lot of useful chord shapes. The chords for this etude are shown below. There is a measure of rest before each chord change to give you time to move your left hand to the new shape.

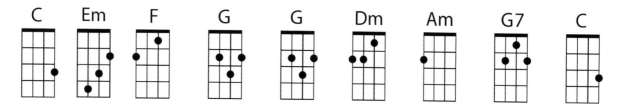

The following chords are new:

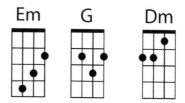

When you're first learning the Etude, you might practice each new change by itself 5 to 7 times until it is easy. For example, you could start with playing C major to E minor. Once you've mastered C to Em, then you could practice Em to F 5 to 7 times. When that progression is flowing a little better, try F to G 5 to 7 times. When you've got F to G working, then try playing C, Em, F, G 5 to 7 times. Continue adding on new changes, one at a time, until you can play the whole series of chords.

Another idea is to leave your ukulele out by the TV or by your bed. You can practice chord changes during commercials or silently while watching a game. 5 or 10 minutes a day will get your left hand used to the new chord changes.

By the way, sometimes ukulele players who don't want to learn the E minor chord or the B flat major chord will substitute the Cmaj7 chord instead.

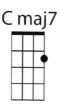

Jenny thinks it doesn't sound quite as good, but Rebecca likes the idea that it can get you through a song that might be too hard otherwise. Also, if you find your hand will not make the more difficult chord shape, it's nice to have a chord shape you can make that still sounds good. We think of it like modifying a yoga pose in a yoga class. Some people are very flexible and some are not. You have to do what is possible for you!

Another possible way to play the E minor chord is shown below:

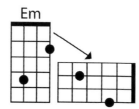

Jenny prefers the three finger version because it will help you get ready to learn the B flat chord, and because the two finger version is often out of tune on soprano ukuleles. Again, it's important to find a fingering that works for you and sounds good. You can always start with learning the chord with one fingering and then switch to a different one later.

Some of you might be wondering *why* there are alternate fingerings for chords. A chord is made up of certain combinations of pitches. For example, the E minor chord is made up of the pitches of E, G, and B. A musician can play the pitches in any order from low to high and it will still sound like an E minor chord.

Also the ukulele has four strings. So when we are playing a three-note chord on the ukulele, we are usually playing one of the chord notes twice with two different strings. One fingering might have you playing E, G, B, G, and another might have you playing G, E, B, E. Both combinations of notes sound like an E minor chord but they have different fingerings.

New Chord Scale Etude

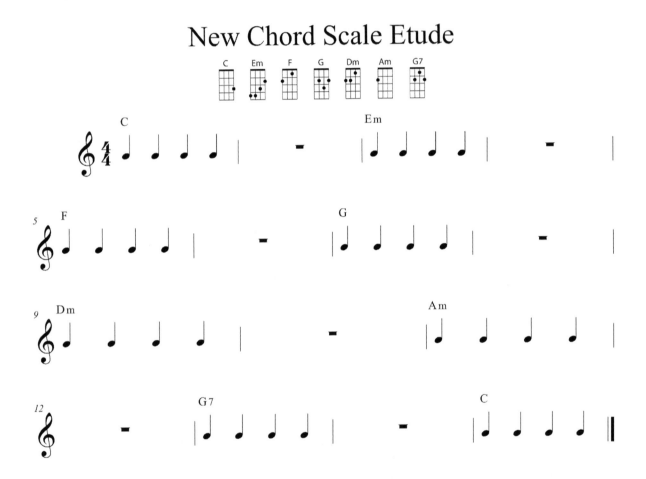

Etude #2–The Fun Descending Scale Etude

Now that you learned something hard, we want to teach you an easier progression that has only one new chord and no three-finger chord shapes. It uses the following chords:

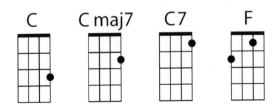

This progression is a great way to learn the Cmaj7 chord. You could also insert the Cmaj7 and C7 chords into a song between C and F chords to make your playing sound more sophisticated. C and F chords often show up together because they are both important chords in the scale of C Major.

The Fun Descending Scale Etude

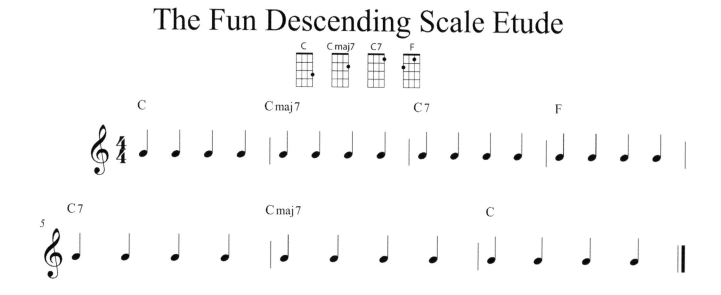

Etude #3–Learning Dominant Chords Etude or the "Five Foot Two" Progression

The next etude for this chapter is the *Learning Dominant Chords Etude*. This chord progression was really popular in the 1920's when the ukulele first became popular. If you want to sound retro, you will need to learn this chord progression. Also, all of these chords show up a lot in ukulele songs!

Super complicated music theory point for you analytical types out there: this chord progression moves through a lot of different scales very fast. That's because each scale has only one dominant chord. So this progression starts in C major, then travels through three scales with the E7, D7, and A7 chords, and then returns to C major via G7 chord. That's because G7 is part of the C major chord family: it is the dominant of C major.

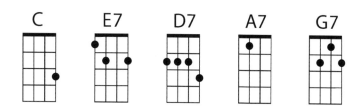

Learning Dominant Chords Etude

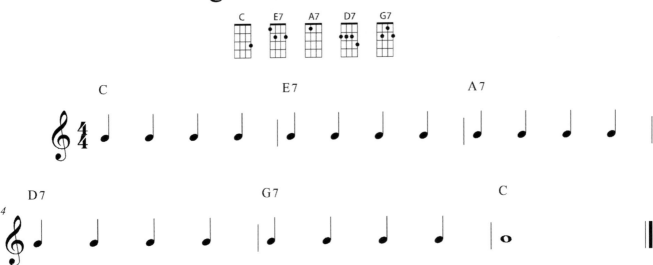

Etude #4–A Minor to G Major

The chord change from A minor to G major occurs in a lot of songs because A minor and G major are both chords of the C major scale. It can be difficult to learn because you have to move your second finger (middle finger) from the string closest to the ceiling to the string closest to the floor very quickly.

We've included *The Lazy Sailor* as a tuneful way to practice this chord change. The original title of this song is *The Drunken Sailor,* but we toned down the lyrics for when children might be present! The A minor to G major change also shows up in *Scarborough Fair*.

You can choose an alternate fingering for this chord change, but we don't recommend it. Because this finger movement comes up often in other songs, it's a good idea to bite the bullet and master it. And learning it will lay the groundwork for you to advance to even harder chord combinations in the future.

The Lazy Sailor

Strumming Pattern:
↓　↓　↓　↓

What do you say to a la-zy sai-lor, what do you say to a la-zy sai-lor,
Shave his bel-ly with a rust-y ra-zor, shave his be-ly with a rust-y ra-zor,

what do you say to a la-zy sai-lor Ear-ly in the morn - ing.
shave his bel-ly with a rust-y ra-zor Ear-ly in the morn - ing.

Put him in a boat and make him bail her. Put him in a boat and make him bail her.
What do you do with a la-zy sai-lor, what do you do with a la-zy sai-lor,

Put him in a boat and make him bail her ear-ly in the morn - ing.
what do you do with a la-zy sai-lor ear-ly in the morn - ing.

Etude #5–A Minor Etude

For any major or minor scale the most important chords are built on the first, fourth and fifth notes of the scale. We used the blues progression to learn these chords in the keys of C, F, G, and D.

Etude #5 will help you learn the most important chords in the key of A minor which are A Minor, D Minor and E7. They are build on the first, fourth and fifth notes of the A minor scale. Knowing these chords means you will be ready to play many songs in A minor.

Previously we talked about the seven notes or pitches of the C Major scale. Now let's learn about the A Minor scale. Why A Minor? Well, because it uses the exact same pitches in the same order as C Major. The only difference is that the A minor scale starts on A and the C major scale starts on C.

Compare the scale pictures shown below. Both scales use the pitches represented by the letters of the alphabet. Both scales use all white keys on the piano. Just like for C major, the eighth note of the A minor scale is the same as the first one. Like C major, A minor is an easy key for the ukulele because it uses so many open strings.

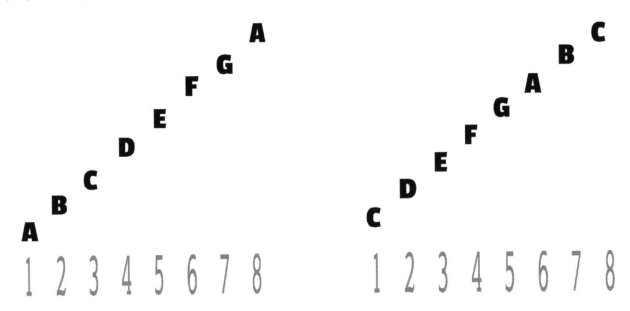

You already have learned many of the chords of the A minor scale because they are the same as the chords for C major. The most commonly seen members of the chord family of the A minor scale are shown below.

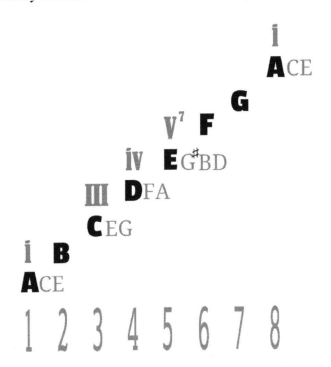

Notice how all the letters that make up the chords are the same as the letters that make up the scale...except one. "Hey wait a minute!" you exclaim. "What is that G# doing in the E7 chord? That is not in the A minor scale you wrote above!"

Very true. The answer is rather complicated. Basically, musicians felt that songs written in minor scales didn't sound good without adding an extra note. In the case of A minor, the extra note is G#, which is used instead of G in some of the chords of the scale of A minor in some songs. The purpose of the G# is to make the V7 chord sound the same as it does in major scales.

If the above paragraph does not make sense to you, don't worry. You don't need to understand the "why" to be able to play songs in A minor. But if you are interested in learning more about music theory, we recommend the following websites:

www.musictheory.net This site has a lot of detailed written-out lessons for you left-brain type learners. It explains the concepts covered above in a lot more detail. It also provides ear training exercises. Be forewarned, though, most of the information is written out in standard music notation.

www.meludia.com This is a new site out of France with beautiful abstract graphics. It has almost no words or music notation – perfect for right-brain learners. It focuses solely on training your ear to distinguish between many different musical sounds, including chord qualities and scales.

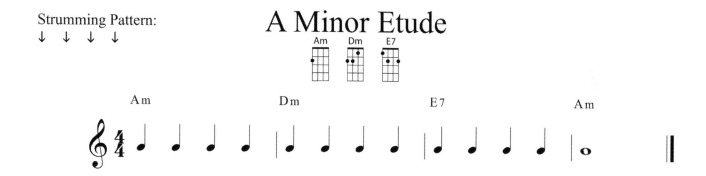

Chapter 4 – Learning New Chords with the Blues

In Chapter 2 you learned two blues scales, how to play the blues using the C, F and G7 chords, and how to improvise over a 12 bar blues progression. You also learned two blues songs, *Lonely Blues* and *New Chord Blues*. Now we're going to play the *New Chord Blues* in different scales, which is called **transposing**. In the process, we'll learn more new chords.

Blues in F Major

The first version of *New Chord Blues* is in F major and uses the B flat Major chord. This chord is one of the most awkward 3 finger chords on the ukulele, so be patient with yourself if you do not get it right away. The B flat chord shape looks like this.

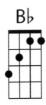

As you can see from the photograph, you will need to put your first finger on two strings at once to master this chord. You will have to experiment with different finger angles and pressures to make sure your first finger is fretting two strings at once. You might try practicing just the first finger position by itself until it is comfortable, or at least sounding good, and then try adding the other fingers. Be sure to check out the lesson video on how to play this chord.

The B flat chord is similar in shape to the E minor chord. If you mastered that chord in the last chapter, the B flat chord will be easier to learn. Practice moving back and forth between E minor and the B flat chord. Their left hand shapes are very similar, so if you can play one of the chords, you can teach yourself to play the other one.

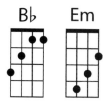

Here is a picture of the F scale and the F triads. Notice that the chords of the F blues progression are built on notes 1, 4 and 5 of the F scale, just like the chords of the C blues progression were built on notes 1, 4 and 5 of the C scale.

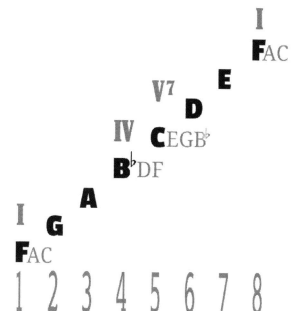

The blues progression in F major goes like this: (At least there is only one new chord!)

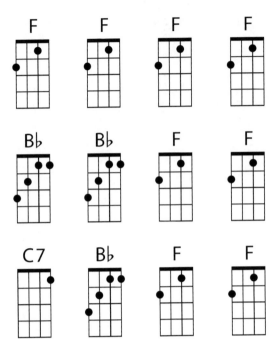

Here is *New Chord Blues* in F Major:

Blues in G Major

Congratulations, you've mastered the F Major blues progression! Next, we'll transpose *New Chord Blues* to G Major, so you can practice the D7 chord. We'll teach you two ways to play the D7 chord.

"Easy" D7

The first version of D7 only uses two fingers. Using this version of D7 makes it much easier to switch to the three finger G chord because the D7 shape is closely related to the G shape. The D7 often occurs right before the G chord because D7 is the V7 chord of the G major scale.

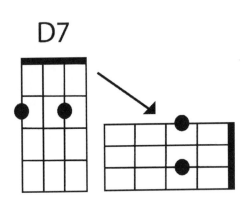

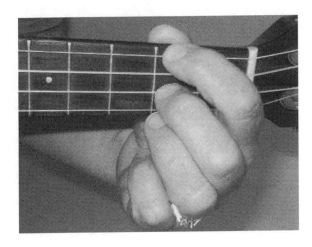

Movable Barre D7

The second version of D7 also uses only two fingers, but you have to flatten your first finger in the second fret so you are stopping three strings with one finger. It can take quite a bit of practice to get comfortable with this flattened finger position, which is referred to as a ***barre*** (or "bar"). The big plus of the D7 barre chord shape is that you can then slide your left hand up and down the fret board and play lots of other similar sounding dominant 7th chords using the same hand shape. Ukulele players refer to this type of chord as a ***movable barre*** chord. You'll learn more about barre chords in Chapter 9 of this book.

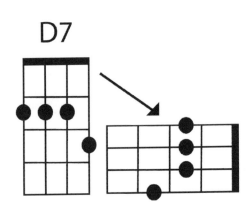

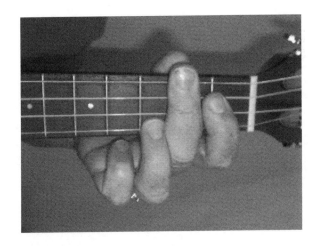

Here is a picture of the G scale and the G triads. Notice that the G blues progression chords of G, D, and D7 are built on notes 1, 4 and 5 of the G scale just as the C blues chords of C, F, and G7 are built on notes 1, 4, and 5 of the C scale.

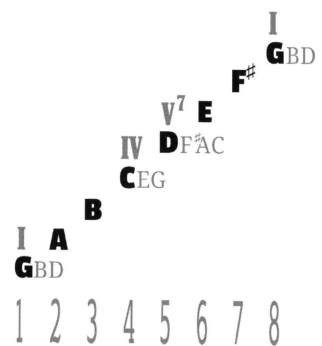

Here is the progression of *New Chord Blues* in G Major.

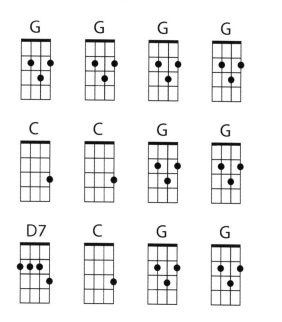

Here is *New Chord Blues* in G Major.

Blues in D Major

The next key is D Major. For this version, you will need to learn the following chords:

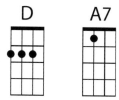

The D Major chord has a new shape. You can finger this chord using three fingers, or use two fingers, or use the first finger as a barre but keep the "A" string open. We prefer to use two fingers for this chord, flattening the knuckle of the second finger, so you can get the finger to lie on two strings. You may find this shape similar to the D Minor and D7 chord shapes, which makes it easier to remember the three different "D" chords. There's a lesson video to help you learn this chord shape.

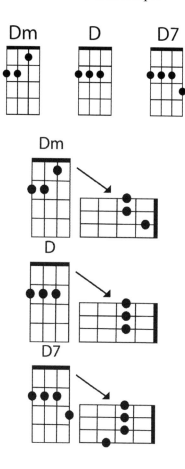

Here is a picture of the D scale and triads so you can see how the D blues progression chords are built on the same notes of the scale (1,4, and 5) as the C blues progression chords.

Here is the chord progression of *New Chord Blues* in the key of D.

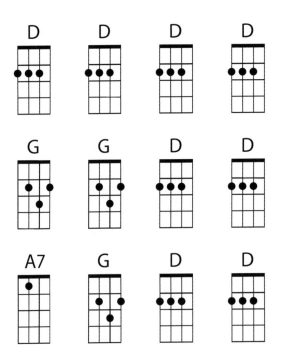

Here is *New Chord Blues* in D Major:

Chapter 5 – Songs in Triple Meter

In this chapter we will introduce a new time signature. Up to now, all of our songs have had four beats in each measure. Most rock, rap and pop songs have four beats to a measure. Musicians call this time signature *quadruple meter*, or just 'simple' or 'common' time.

Now we will introduce songs that have three beats in the measure. We call this kind of rhythmic organization *triple meter*. Since close to 95 percent of the music we hear is in quadruple meter, expect triple meter to feel different and take a while to learn. We are starting with a well-known song with easy chords to help you get used to triple meter.

On Top of Old Smokey has a lot of verses, so you can play and sing the same chords and melody many times to practice this new meter. We will use chords you already know in our rendition of this song. A version you might know is *On Top of Spaghetti.* Feel free to substitute these lyrics if you like them better.

Start strumming on the first beat of the first full measure, underneath the G chord shape. When you begin, play three down strokes per measure (D, D, D). When you are more comfortable, you can try adding the up strum on beat two of each measure (D, DU, D).

Next let's revisit the timeless favorite *Amazing Grace*. Again, if the down, down-up, down strumming pattern is too hard, just do three down strums per measure.

Amazing Grace was published in 1779 by John Newton (1725-1807). Newton learned to sail with his father and then enlisted as a crew member on a merchant vessel. Soon after his enlistment he was forced to serve in the British Royal Navy, a common practice at the time. He tried to escape the Navy but was caught and flogged in front of the ship's crew. Eventually he was able to transfer to another ship, but the crew did not like him. They left him in West Africa with a slave dealer who gave Newton to an African princess. The princess abused and mistreated Newton alongside her other slaves.

In 1748 a sea captain sent by his father rescued him. On his voyage home to England he awoke to find the ship filling with water during a violent storm. Just as he called out to God for mercy the cargo shifted enough to stop the leak, and he was saved from drowning. He later wrote that his spiritual conversion began at this moment. As he grew more committed to his Christian faith he came to believe that the slave trade was wrong. He became a prominent abolitionist and evangelical religious leader and was influential in Britain's abolition of slavery in 1807.

Another well-known song in triple meter is *A Bicycle Built for Two.* In the late 19th century when this song was first written, bicycles were a modern and liberating form of transportation. Suffragettes rode bicycles, and many young men had great adventures circumnavigating the globe. The League of American Cyclists was the first group in the United States to argue for the improvement of roads between cities.

Daisy seems to be reacting against some of the freedoms a bicycle can bring when she tells Michael that "I'll be switched if I'll be hitched to a bicycle built for two." (By "switched" she means beaten with a flexible stick. Apparently Daisy was not a suffragette.)

Strumming Pattern:
↓ ↓↑ ↓

On Top of Old Smokey

Amazing Grace

Bicycle Built for Two

Chapter 6 – Songs in Minor Mode

Do you remember the minor chords you learned in Chapter 3 with the *New Chord Scale Etude* and the *A Minor Chords Etude?* Now you get to use them in four beautiful minor key songs.

Wayfarin' Stranger is a traditional American folk song that is both mournful and joyous. It tells of the difficult journey through life on our way to "that bright world." Like most folk songs, its origins depend on who you ask – some say it's a reworked African-American spiritual, while others say it was brought to America by the Scotch-Irish settlers of Appalachia. Burl Ives first popularized it in 1944, and it's also been recorded by Pete Seeger, Joan Baez, Johnny Cash, Emmylou Harris, and Allison Krauss.

When Johnny Comes Marching Home is an American folk song dating from the time of the Revolutionary War. It tells the story of a soldier returning home from battle, with lyrics as relevant today as they were 240 years ago.

In *Scarborough Fair* the singer tells the listener to ask his former love to do a series of impossible tasks. If she makes him a shirt without a seam and washes it in a dry well, he will take her back. Often the song is sung as a duet, with the woman then giving her lover a series of equally impossible tasks, promising to give him his seamless shirt once he has finished.

Wait a minute! Isn't this song by Simon and Garfunkel? Not exactly. Versions of this ballad have been traced back as far as 1670. Over the years, it was modified, and rewritten so that dozens of versions existed by the end of the 18th century. The references to "Scarborough Fair" and the refrain "parsley, sage, rosemary, and thyme" date to 19th century versions.

Paul Simon learned the song from Martin Carthy, who had picked it up from a songbook by Ewan MacColl and Peggy Seeger. It was the lead track of the 1966 album "Parsley, Sage, Rosemary and Thyme" and was released as a single after being featured in the *The Graduate* in 1968. The adult content of the film was considered shocking at the time, which gave Simon and Garfunkel's career a boost even though the soundtrack is definitely rated "G."

The House of the Rising Sun is a traditional folk song, sometimes called *Rising Sun Blues*. It tells of a life gone wrong in New Orleans. Like many classic folk ballads, the authorship of this song is uncertain. Music historians say that it is based on traditional 18th century English ballads and travelled to America with English immigrants where it was later adapted to its New Orleans setting.

Folks disagree on the building or place *House of the Rising Sun* refers to. Some say it's about the slave pens of a plantation, the plantation house itself, a prison, a brothel, or a treatment clinic for prostitutes with syphilis.

The oldest known recording of the song was made in 1934. The song was among those collected by folklorist Alan Lomax on his 1937 tour of Appalachia with a primitive set of recording equipment to capture the American folk songs of the region.

The most successful commercial version was recorded in 1964 by the English rock group The Animals. Many other artists have recorded the song, including Bob Dylan and Joan Baez, Woody Guthrie, Leadbelly, Roy Acuff, Glen Yarbrough, Andy Griffith, Miriam Makeba, Dolly Parton and Nina Simone.

When Johnny Comes Marching Home

Strumming Pattern:
↓ ↑↓ ↑↓ ↑↓ ↑

Wayfaring Stranger

Strumming Pattern:
↓ ↓↑ ↓ ↓↑

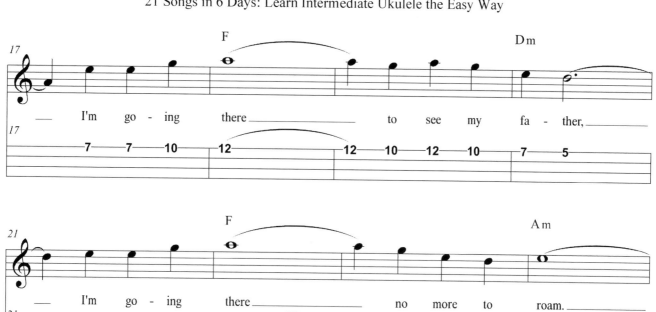

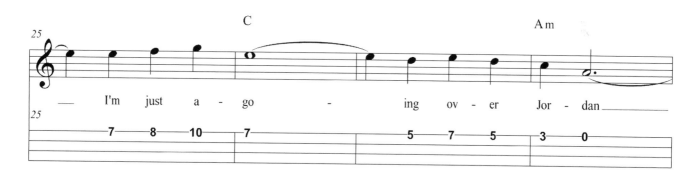

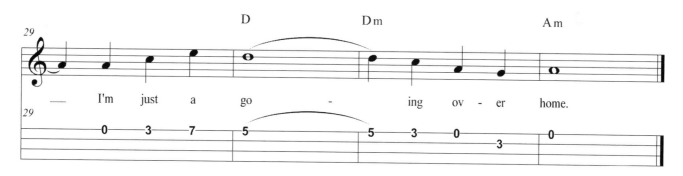

Scarborough Fair

Strumming Pattern:
↓ ↓↑ ↓

The House of the Rising Sun

Chapter 7 – Fancy Strums

Music must have rhythm. To quote Duke Ellington: "It don't mean a thing, if it ain't got that swing." Often the hardest part of a song is its timing, rather than its chords. On the ukulele, it's your strumming that creates the beat or swing of the music.

In this chapter, you'll learn more complicated strumming patterns. They will be written in standard musical notation beneath the melody, so you can *see* how the strumming pattern fits with the words of the songs.

How to Practice Strumming

If you have been struggling with strumming, don't worry. Developing your ability to coordinate two hands with your voice in a precisely timed way can be a tricky business. It may take a bit of slow, patient practice before you develop a solid sense of beat. So to speed matters along, here is a practice regimen to get your strumming up to speed.

Be sure to use your index finger or all the fingers of the right hand on the down strum. Do *not* use the thumb for down strums, because learning to add the other fingers later is difficult. The best ukulele players use all four of their fingers and their right thumb to create a wide variety of strummed, picked, and hammered sounds.

- Start with all down strums. Stay on one easy chord with your left hand or strum open strings.

- Next, add the up strums. First try Strum 2, equally spaced down and up strums.

- Then try Strum 3, with an uneven division of the beat.

- Gradually increase the tempo, so you can strum more quickly. The increase in speed should be almost imperceptible to you – about 4 to 8 metronome points at a time.

Practicing Strumming with a Metronome

A metronome will give you a rock steady beat that you can match your strums to. A metronome will also make it easier to increase tempo very, very gradually. Most new learners try to increase their playing speed much too quickly. Remember, when you are learning strumming, only increase your speed by 4 to 8 points on the metronome at a time.

There is no excuse not to try a metronome. There are lots of free metronome apps out there for your smart phone or tablet. Some of the Snark tuners also have built in metronomes.
YouTube has some great videos showing how to play with a metronome. Try searching on 'metronome

ukulele' to find some you can play along with. We've put a few of our favorites in the members' area of ukulele.io.

One of the things musicians like about metronomes is that they work like speedometers – they serve as a way to measure exactly how fast you are going. They can be very helpful for communicating the precise speed to play a song. Rebecca had a church job where she played hymns on the piano as a duet with a fabulous organist who had been an arranger for the Army band in the 1940's. Every week the organist (let's call him John) would send a Rebecca long email. Needless to say, John did NOT own a metronome:

"OK, for 'Now Thank We All Our God,' we'll do the first verse as written – you play the melody in octaves, I'll play chords. Next verse, play in the key of D flat instead of C major. You do rippling broken chords and I'll play the melody with the flute stop. Tempo is the same as 'Yes We Have No Bananas.'"

Hate Metronomes? Other Ways to Practice Strumming

Find a song video you like on YouTube and strum along with the artist. You probably won't be able to keep up with both strumming and chord changes, so stop the strings with your left hand and practice strumming along without making any chord shapes.

Next, add the chord changes in the song, but simply strum down strums on the beat. Gradually upgrade to a more complicated pattern until you master the relationship between the left and right hands. Practice this skill 10 minutes a day, and you will see great improvement over time.

You can strum along with YouTube videos on that have great backup beats. Find them by searching on terms like uke backing tracks, ukulele blues backing tracks, and best uke backing tracks. Links which say they are for guitar will also work for ukulele. There are videos at many different speeds you can use develop your right hand patterns. You can choose rock from rock, hip-hop, disco, and many other styles. Play with a different video every day and pretty soon your strumming will be automatic and consistent.

Joining a ukulele club is a fun way to improve your strumming. Clubs sing and strum songs together, and most clubs also offer some instruction. Strumming in a group will help you learn to be steady and you may even be more inspired to practice!

Time for Some Songs

Our first song is *The Lazy Sailor.* You already learned it in in Chapter 3 with all down strums. Now you can add a fancier strumming pattern.

Swing Low, Sweet Chariot is a spiritual written by two slaves, Wallace and Minerva Willis. Their owner, Brit Willis, took them along the Trail of Tears to Oklahoma's Indian Territory where he rented them to the Spencer Academy for Choctaw Indian boys. The couple sang *Chariot* for the students, and the school's headmaster was so impressed that he sent the song to the Fisk Jubilee Singers of Fisk University in Nashville. The Singers took the song on tour in the United States and Europe and performed it for Queen Victoria in England. The song's popularity endured, and a hundred years later, Joan Baez performed it at Woodstock.

Michael, Row the Boat Ashore is another slave-era spiritual transcribed by abolitionist Charles Pickard Ware. He visited plantations on St. Helena Island off the South Carolina coast during the Civil War to help the black freedmen whose owners had abandoned the island to escape the Union navy. This song uses the same strumming pattern as *Swing Low, Sweet Chariot*.

Oh, Susanna was written by Stephen Foster (1826-1864). Foster wrote more than 200 songs but this one was the most popular. The Forty-Niners who followed the Gold Rush adopted the song created new lyrics about traveling to California with a "washpan on my knee." Since many of the lyrics are already nonsense, why not make up some of your own? This song also uses the down, down-up, down, down-up strum.

The Erie Canal depicts early 19th century life on the canal which ran through New York from the Hudson River to Lake Erie. Boats were towed by mules, and each time the boat passed under a bridge everyone had to duck. Pete Seeger and the Kingston Trio recorded versions of *Erie Canal*. Use Strum 3 for this song. The lesson video will help you feel the rhythm of this strumming pattern, which is often called "Swung 8ths".

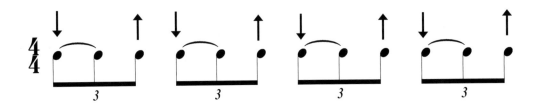

Won't You Come Home Bill Bailey was written in 1902 by Detroit-born songwriter Hughie Cannon, who also wrote *Frankie and Johnny*. Over the years it's been recorded by a wide range of artists, including Louis Armstrong, Patsy Cline, Bobby Darin, Aretha Franklin, Jimmy Durante, and Phish. The down, down-up, up-down-up strum gives this song has a wonderful jazz feel. And since it has very few chord changes, it's a good song for mastering this new strumming pattern.

Our final song of this chapter, *You Are My Sunshine,* is an American country music song of unknown authorship. First recorded in 1939 by Jimmie Davis and Charles Mitchell, it was also recorded by Bing Crosby, Lawrence Welk, Nat King Cole, Ray Charles, Ike and Tina Turner, Aretha Franklin, Johnny Cash, Brian Wilson, and Andy Williams. The song was brought home to its country beginnings in the 2000 film, *O Brother, Where Art Thou?* with a performance by guitar virtuoso Norman Blake.

The Lazy Sailor

Swing Low, Sweet Chariot

Strumming Pattern:
↓ ↓↑ ↓ ↓↑

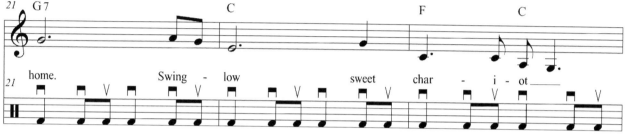

Michael Row the Boat Ashore

Strumming Pattern:
↓ ↓↑ ↓ ↓↑

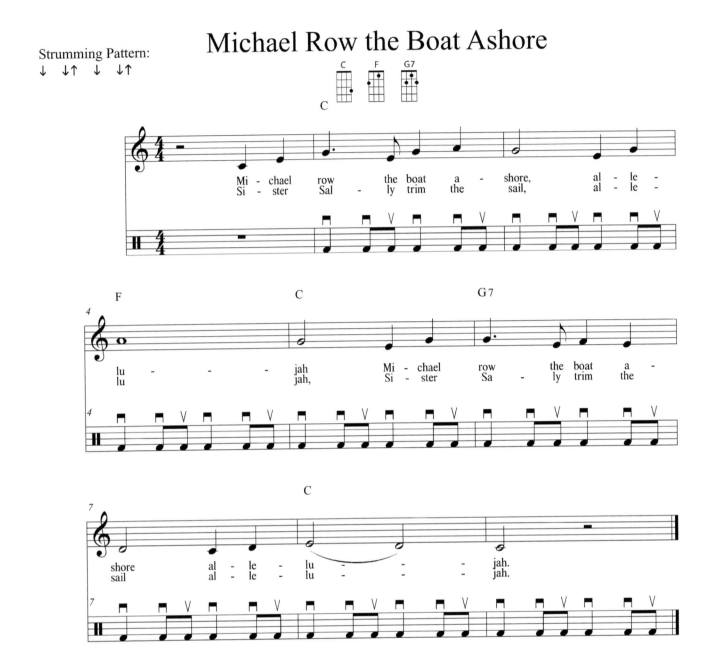

Stumming Pattern:
↓ ↓↑ ↑↓↑

You Are My Sunshine

Oh Susanna

Strumming Pattern:
↓ ↓↑ ↓ ↓↑

VERSE 3:
I soon will be in New Orleans, and then I'll look around,
And when I find Susanna, I'll fall upon the ground.
But if I do not find her, then I will surely die,
And when I'm dead and buried, Oh, Susanna, don't you cry.
CHORUS

The Erie Canal

Strumming Pattern: Swung 8ths
↓   ↓   ↑↓   ↓↑

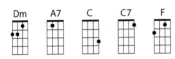

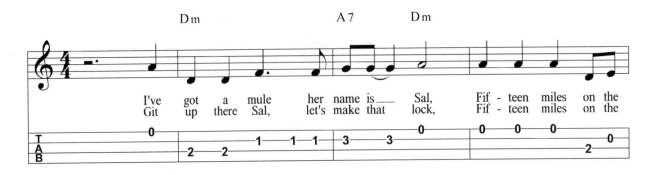

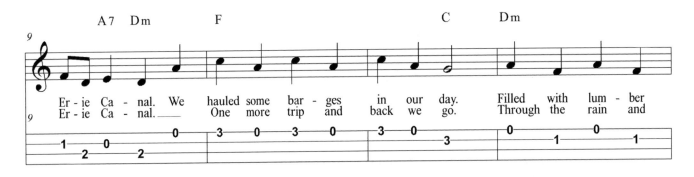

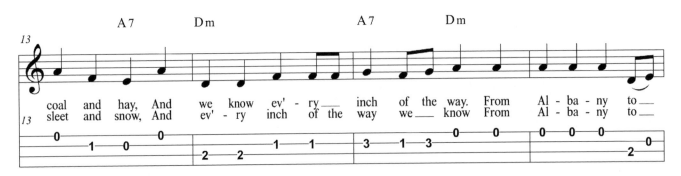

Won't You Come Home Bill Bailey

Hughie Canon

Jenny Peters

Chapter 8 – Fingerpicking Accompaniments

In this chapter, you'll learn a beautiful alternative to strumming: fingerpicking chords on the ukulele. We've written out the fingerpicking accompaniment in both standard music and tab notation below the lyrics so you can use it to help you learn fingerpicking more quickly.

Fingerpicking in Quadruple Meter

Are You Sleeping? is the first song with a fingerpicking accompaniment. Because it has only one chord you can completely ignore your left hand and concentrate on getting your right hand to pluck the correct strings.

Use your thumb for the two strings closest to the ceiling and the index and middle fingers for the two strings closest to the floor. Pluck the outer strings and then the inner ones in a pinching motion. Saying "out, out, in, in; out, out, in, in" will help your fingers get the right pattern for each measure.

Twinkle, Twinkle Little Star is our next song. It uses the same "out, out, in, in" fingerpicking pattern. But because *Twinkle* has three chords, you'll have to coordinate your left hand's chord changes with the right hand's fingerpicking assignment.

Fingerpicking in Triple Meter

Here's the pattern for fingerpicking in triple meter (three beats per measure):

- On beat one of the measure pluck the outer two strings
- On beats two and three pluck the inner two strings

Thinking "out, out, in, in, in, in" will help you can track of which strings to pluck when.

Take a look at the music for *Amazing Grace* with a fingerpicking accompaniment. Here's how to use the music notation to help you keep track of the fingerpicking pattern for triple meter and to see how the pattern fits with the melody and lyrics.

The fingerpicking pattern is written on the note staff below the lyrics. Notice that the notes are grouped in pairs, and that the first pair of notes is on a different line or space than pairs two and three. Also, pairs two and three are always the same. That's because of the "out, out, in, in, in, in" pattern.

It's even easier to see the fingerpicking pattern on the tab staff. Remember that the lines of the tab staff represent the ukulele strings. The first two numbers of each measure are on the top and bottom lines of the tab staff which represent the outer strings. The last four numbers of each measure are on the middle two lines of the tab staff which represent the inner strings.

Now compare the staves vertically. The top staff represents the melody sounds, and the bottom two staves represent the fingerpicked accompaniment. When two notes or a number on the tab staff line up directly above one another, it means that those two sounds happen at the same time. Use this vertical alignment to understand precisely how the melody fits with what your hands are doing. You'll learn this new skill more quickly when you know the exact timing of what you are trying to do.

Scarborough Fair is our second song in triple meter. The fingerpicked chords give this song a delicate English Renaissance sound. Simon and Garfunkel's 1968 recording of the song uses a fingerpicked guitar accompaniment.

Are You Sleeping
Fingerpicking Accompaniment

C

Are you sleep - ing, are you sleep - ing? Bro - ther John, Bro - ther John?

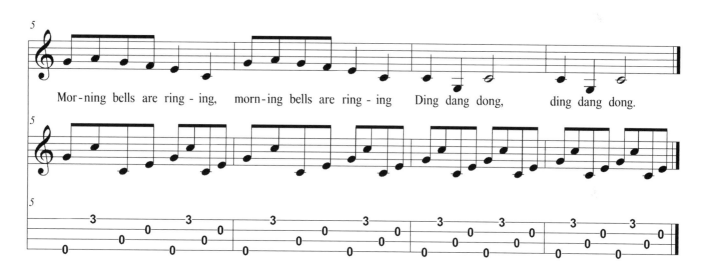

Mor - ning bells are ring - ing, morn - ing bells are ring - ing Ding dang dong, ding dang dong.

Twinkle, Twinkle Little Star Melody

Fingerpicking Accompaniment

Amazing Grace
Fingerpicking Accompaniment

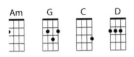

Scarborough Fair
Fingerpicking Accompaniment

Chapter 9 – Solo Ukulele with Chord Melodies

In this chapter you'll learn how to play solo ukulele using chord melodies. What that means is that you will play the melody and the chords of the song at the same time on your ukulele. NO singing!

Jake Shimabakuro uses this type of playing when he plays his transcriptions of *While My Guitar Gently Weeps* and *Bohemian Rhapsody.* We won't be teaching you anything that complicated. But playing chord melodies is quite rewarding, because the songs actually sound like songs complete with melody, harmony and rhythm. And it's fun to imitate the ukulele greats.

You'll need to read tab to learn these chord melodies from the written notation. Not so strong at reading tab? Review Chapter 1 as needed. You can also watch the lesson videos to help you hear and see how the song should go.

Barre Chords in First, Second and Third Position

Below is a picture of Jenny's left hand playing an F Major barre chord in the first, second, and third positions. You will use a barre chord for solo ukulele chord melodies.

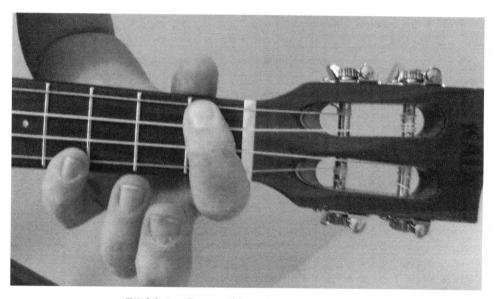

C# Major Barre Chord in First Position

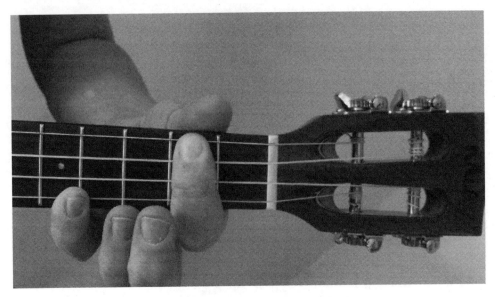

D Major Barre Chord in Second Position

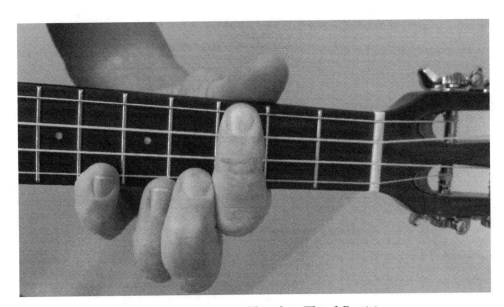

E Flat Major Barre Chord in Third Position

Our first song is *Oh When The Saints.* It stays in the first position, so it's not too difficult. And since you have played this song before, your ear and hands already know a lot of its patterns. Use your thumb to pluck the melody notes and the fingers on your right hand to strum the chords. This way the melody is louder than the chords. You can tell which notes are melody notes because they have lyrics under them.

Amazing Grace is our second song. You might remember from Chapters 1 and 5 that this melody requires your left hand to change position often. Since it is in the key of C you can use open strings for many of the harmony notes, which makes the chords are less difficult than they would be in another key. Use your thumb to play the melody note with a louder sound and then all the fingers of your right hand to strum the chords more quietly. Jenny put the chords on the second beat of the measure after the melody note to give you time to switch between thumb and fingers.

Aura Lee is our third solo ukulele song. Elvis Presley used this melody in *Love Me Tender*. In this chord melody you'll need to pluck melody and accompaniment notes with one downward motion. We suggest you use your thumb for these combined melody and accompaniment sounds. Use your right hand fingers to lightly strum all four strings when there is no melody note to play.

Our final song is *Aloha O'e,* sometimes called *Farewell to Thee.* This traditional Hawaiian song was written in 1878 by Queen Lili'uokalani, the last Hawaiian monarch. The story goes that she was horseback riding and saw a young couple embracing beside the water. They inspired her to write Aloha O'e as a love song. When Hawai'i was annexed to the United States in 1923, she rewrote the song as a farewell to her native land. Lili'uokalani's handwritten manuscript and musical score are preserved in the Hawai'i State Archives.

Aloha O'e involves shifting all over the ukulele. Although there are a few barre chords, they are not too difficult.

Have fun with these songs!

Oh, When The Saints for Solo Ukulele

Arr. Jenny Peters

Aura Lee

Amazing Grace Solo Ukulele

Aloha Oe

Conclusion

We hope you have enjoyed learning intermediate ukulele the easy way!

We'd love to see you on Facebook at facebook.com/21Songsin6Days, on YouTube at ukulele.io/visitYoutube, or hear from you at ukulele.io/contact-us. You can find our complete contact information in *About the Authors*.

Chord Glossary

A

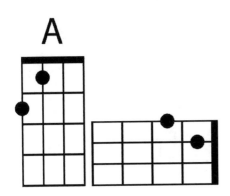

Am

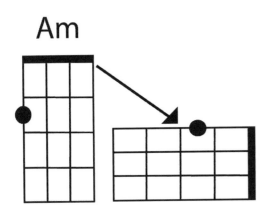

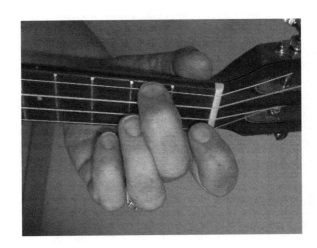

B♭

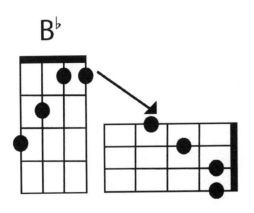

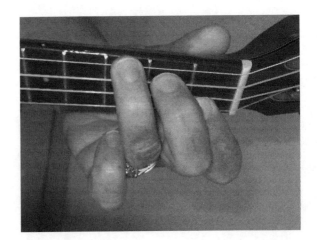

C

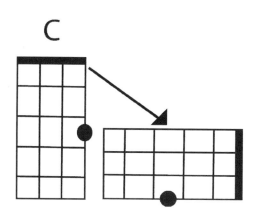

C7

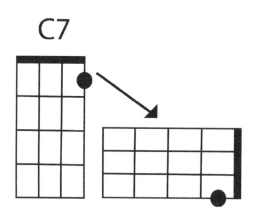

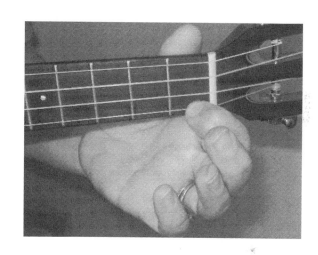

D

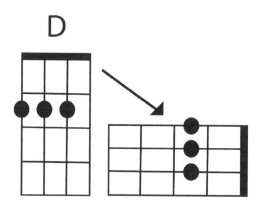

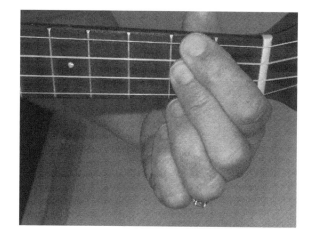

D7

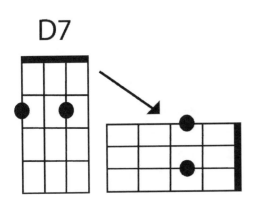

D7

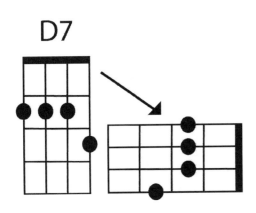

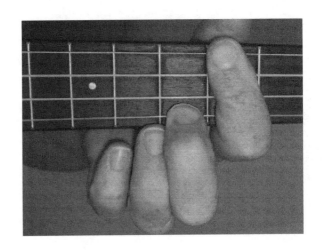

Dm

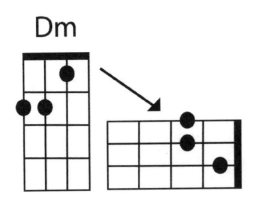

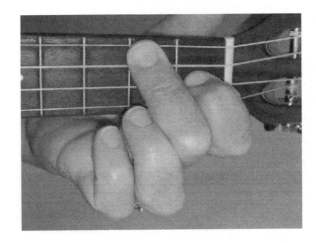

E7

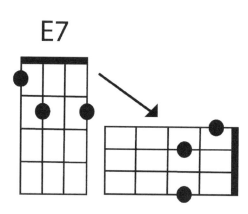
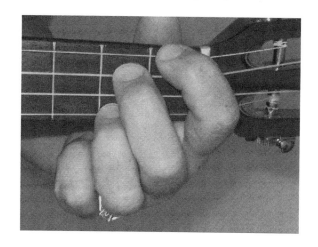

Em

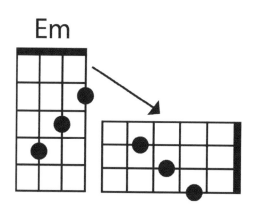
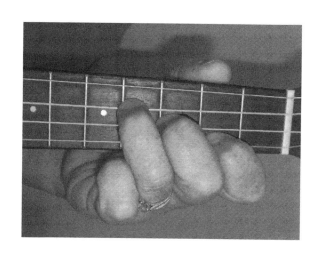

Em

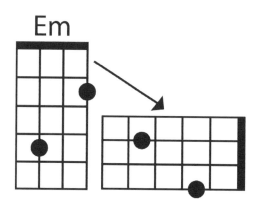
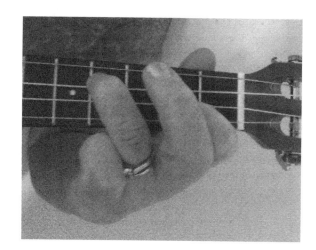

F

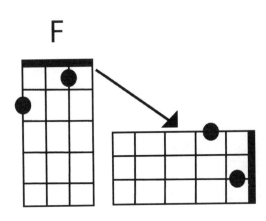

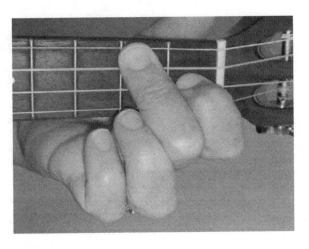

G

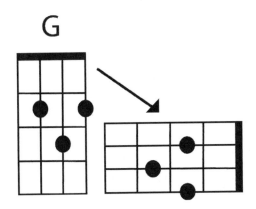

G7

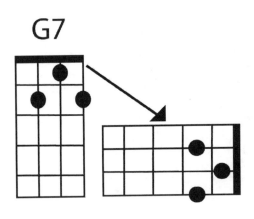

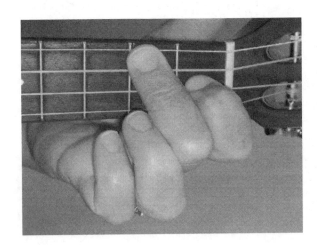

Glossary

Accidental - a *flat, sharp* or *natural*.

Bar - same as a *measure*. A measure is the space on a musical staff between two bar lines. Every measure begins with a strong beat.

Bar lines - the vertical lines on the musical and tab staffs that go from the top line of the staff to the bottom line of the staff. Bar lines are longer than note stems and do not touch any notes.

Barre or bar - using one or more fingers to stop multiple strings on the fretboard. Usually this is done with the index finger.

Barre chord - a chord that contains a *barre*.

Beat - regularly timed sounds that occur the same distance apart in time in a row. Examples of sounds with a beat are the sound your heart makes, i.e. a heartbeat, or the sound of someone dribbling a basketball.

Blue notes - a note or group of notes that are different than the notes used in Western folk music. Usually in the blues we play the different note near its next door note so our ears can imagine the note that belongs in the African scale. In staff notation, a blue note will have a flat, sharp or natural in front of it.

Blues scale - a group of musical sounds that are spaced in the specific way that is used in blues music. The blues scale probably came with African people to the United States. For the blues songs in this book we are playing in the key of C, which is the same as all the white keys on the piano. When we add a black key to the white key scale, the music sounds different. The black key, for example, E flat, added in on top of the white key, such as E, gives the music a bluesy feel. The added black key notes are an attempt to approximate African scales. Western folk music tends to use 8 notes per octave, while African folk music tends to use 5 notes equally spaced per octave. Some of these African scale notes do not exist in Western musical instruments. For example, if you look at a piano keyboard, you can see that there ARE five black keys but the spaces between them are not equal. Thus, when you sing or play a flat note and somebody else is playing a regular note, your ear hears the sound the flat note and the regular note make together as bluesy.

Braguinha - a Portuguese fretted string instrument, like a small guitar, that was an ancestor of the ukulele.

Cavaquinho - another Portuguese fretted string instrument like the braguinha.

Chord

Chord progression - order of chords in a song.

Chord stamp - a symbol or drawing of the ukulele strings with little dots that represent where to place your fingers on the fretboard to make the chord.

Clef - A clef is a musical symbol used to indicate the pitch of the notes written on the staff. It is always shown at the beginning of each line or stave of music. See also *treble clef*.

Etude - a piece of music that is designed to help you learn and practice a new musical skill. In French, etude means study so etudes are sometimes called studies.

Finger numbers - these are applied to the left hand. Finger 1 is the index or "pointer" finger; finger 2 is the middle finger; finger 3 is the ring finger; and finger 4 is the pinky. For playing ukulele, we do not count the thumb because it is behind the neck of the ukulele and not available to stop a string (see "stopping").

First position - means your finger 1 (index finger) is in the first fret, the one closest to the tuning pegs.

Flat - a musical symbol placed in front of musical note. It means to lower the sound slightly, by the amount that musicians call a "half step." When you look at a blues scale, you can see a little sign that looks like a small letter "b" next to some of the notes. That sign is called is a flat and it lowers the pitch of the note by one-half step.

Fretboard - the long skinny part of the ukulele with metal strips in it. It is usually made of a different color wood than the larger curvy part of the instrument.

Fretting - pushing the strings against the fretboard with the fingers of your left hand so each note you play sounds clear. "Fretting" means the same thing as "stopping."

Frets - strips of metal that run across the short dimension of the long skinny fretboard. When you push down a string with your finger in between the frets, the string is held very tightly against the fret.

Guitar - a large fretted string instrument. It usually has six or more strings in comparison to the ukulele's four strings.

Improvisation - Musical improvisation means to make up music as you are playing.

Key - short for "key signature," which is a group of flats or sharps at the beginning of each line of written music. The key signature matches up to a specific group of sounds that sound good together. These sounds have precise relationships with one another, and a name: "scale." Usually the name of the key is the same as the name of the chord that starts or ends the song. In most folk and pop music the starting and ending chords are the same.

Lead sheet - a way of writing out a song without using notes on a musical staff to show the pitches of the melody. Instead, the words are written out with chord stamps above them. You have to learn the melody of the song from hearing it sung to be able to use a lead sheet of a song.

Machete - another small guitar-like instrument like the braguinha, cavaquinho, and rajão.

Major - a type of chord. The distances between the pitches of a major chord make it sound happy or bright to most people.

Measure - the space on a musical staff between two bar lines. Every measure begins with a strong beat.

Melody - notes played one at time, one after the other.

Minor - another type of chord. The pitch relationships of a minor chord make it sound dark or sad to most people.

Musical improvisation - to make up music as you are playing.

Natural - a musical symbol placed in front of a musical note. It cancels any sharp or flat symbol that would normally apply to that note.

Note - a round symbol that is placed on a line or space of a musical staff. Some notes are circles or ovals; other types of notes are circles or ovals with lines attached. The circle or oval part of the note can be filled in (solid black) or left empty (white). This circle or oval is called the note head. Each note represents one sound. The color (either black or white) of the note head combined with the stem (the vertical line) indicates how long each sound should last. Sometimes the word "note" is used to refer to just the sounds. For example, you might say, "she played a lot of notes in that song."

Nut - the raised ridge at the top of the ukulele fretboard. It holds the strings slightly away from the fretboard so they can vibrate.

Octave - distance to the same letter note, either higher or lower. You might hear an octave in action when your mom and dad sing the same note and your dad's voice is lower and your mom's is higher but they both sound like they are singing the same note. In Western folk music we have eight notes in an octave. "Oct" means "eight." Two other examples of words that use "oct" to mean eight are octagon and octopus.

Octave transposition – Rewriting a song's melody so it goes up, rather than down, so ukuleles without a "low G" tuning can play it.

Pickup - a pickup means the music begins on a weak beat instead of a strong beat. Almost all music is organized into patterns of strong and weak beats. One very common pattern is strong-weak-weak-weak. Almost all the songs in this book use this pattern. Another common pattern is strong-weak-weak. *Amazing Grace* uses this pattern.

Pitch - whether a sound is high or low. An example of a high sound would be birds tweeting. An example of a low sound would be a thunderstorm.

Pluck - pulling your right (strumming) hand finger against a string firmly and then gradually releasing it so the string vibrates and you hear a nice clear musical sound.

Rajão - a Portuguese fretted string instrument, similar to a small guitar. Braguinha, cavaquinho and machete are other similar instruments.

Rhythm - how sounds make patterns in time. For example, a rainstorm has a different rhythm than a rooster crowing.

Round - a song that can be sung by two groups or two people starting at different times. This way of singing doesn't work with just any song – the song needs to have been written so that it will sound good when different parts of it are overlapped.

Scale - a ladder of musical notes arranged in a specific pattern, usually with small distances in pitch, all going up or down. The names of some common types of scales in Western music are major, minor, and blues. There are hundreds of types of scales in the world.

Second position - means your finger 1 (index finger) is in the second fret, one fret away from the tuning pegs.

Sharp - a musical symbol placed in front of musical note. It means to raise the sound slightly, by the amount that musicians call a "half step."

Stopping - pushing a string against the fretboard with a finger of your left hand so that one end of the string rests against a fret. The other end of the string is tied to the bridge below the sound hole. We say the fret is "stopping" the string because the string can't vibrate where it is being pushed onto the fret. The contact with the fret shortens the amount of the string that is vibrating. Only the part of the string that is in the air and not touching anything is free to vibrate.

Sound hole - round hole in the body of the ukulele.

Staff - a musical staff is made of five equally spaced horizontal lines. There are four spaces. Each line and space of the musical staff represents a specific musical pitch. A tab staff is also made of equally spaced horizontal lines but there are four instead of five for the ukulele. See "tab staff."

Stem - a vertical line attached to the round part of a musical note. The stem helps indicate the rhythm of the note. Note stems are shorter than bar lines and are attached directly to a round note symbol.

String numbers - ukulele strings are numbered from the floor to the ceiling when you are holding the uke in playing position. That means the string closest to your eyes is string 4 with a pitch of G. String 3 has a pitch of C. String 2 has a pitch of E, and string 1 is closest to the floor and has a pitch of A.

Strum 1 - downward strums with a steady beat. Another way to think of it is down strums with equal time between each strum so that the strums sound evenly spaced in time.

Strum 2 - even down-up strokes played with a steady beat. This means there is an equal amount of time between each down and up strum so they sound evenly spaced in time.

Strum 3 - down-up strokes to a steady beat, but the time after the down stroke is longer than the time after the up stroke. Some of the songs in this book such as *Row, Row, Row Your Boat* and *Oats, Peas, Beans, and Barley Grow* use a 6/8 time signature. The pattern of beats in 6/8 time is STRONG-weak-weak STRONG-weak-weak. Usually when we strum a song with a 6/8 time signature we use Strum 3. We do a down strum on the STRONG and an up strum on the second weak beat just before the next STRONG. Most listeners will hear this music as having steady beats that are unevenly divided. Your feeling when you play will be long-short long-short. This long-short pattern is the feeling of Strum 3.

Tablature, or tab staff - a staff especially for fretted stringed instruments including the ukulele. Each line represents one string of the ukulele. There are numbers on the tab staff that tell the player which fret to stop the string on.

Transpose – To play music originally in one scale in a different scale.

Treble clef – A clef is a musical symbol used to indicate the pitch of the notes written on the staff. It is always shown at the beginning of each line or stave of music. The treble clef is also known as the G clef and it indicates that the second line up from the bottom of the staff is G4, the same pitch as the ukulele G string (with standard ukulele tuning.)

Third position - means your finger 1 (index finger) is in the third fret, two frets away from the tuning pegs.

Time signature - the numbers at the beginning of each song on the staff immediately to the right of the clef. It tells you how many beats are in each measure and what the pattern of strong and weak beats is in the song. The 4/4 time signature has the pattern strong-weak-weak-weak. The 3/4 time signature has the pattern strong-weak-weak. The 6/8 time signature has the pattern STRONG-weak-weak STRONG-weak-weak. Every measure begins with a strong beat.

Tuning pegs - located just beyond the nut. Each string is wound around a tuning peg. You can change the pitch of the string by turning the peg to tighten or loosen the string. Tightening the string makes the pitch go higher (a sound more like birds chirping or a girl's voice). Loosening the string makes the pitch go down (a sound more like thunderstorm or a man's voice).

Transposing - playing or singing music starting on a different pitch but keeping the same sound of the melody and chords. When we transpose music, we change what is called the "key."

Work song - a song people sing while working to help them stay together or to express their feelings about their job.

Recommended Reading

Here are some other great ukulele resources to check out:

21 Songs in 6 Days: Learn Ukulele the Easy Way by Rebecca Bogart and Jenny Peters: Learn five basic chords (C, C7, F, G7 and Am) and three fundamental strumming patterns by working through the six days and 40-plus lesson videos.

21 Songs in 6 Days Classroom Edition: Teacher Manual and 21 Songs in 6 Days Classroom Edition: Student Book by Rebecca Bogart and Jenny Peters: includes a teacher manual, student book and complete audio/video teaching curriculum. Designed so you can successfully teach kids (grades 4-8) how to play the ukulele in as little as 30 minutes a week. Includes melody tabs and dedicated chapter on blues improvisation.

21 Easy Ukulele Songs for Christmas by Rebecca Bogart and Jenny Peters: Great sounding yet easy to play versions of seasonal favorites beginning ukulele players who have learned the C, F, and G7 chords and a few basic strums. Includes online lesson videos.

Easy Ukulele Songs: Five with Five Chords by Rebecca Bogart and Jenny Peters: Continue playing five chord songs and tab melodies year round with this short book. Comes with 10 lesson videos to help you learn the songs.

Ukulele Mastery Simplified by Erich Andreas: Now that you've finished our book, you should be able to tackle the three-chord songs that begin this book.

Ukulele For Dummies by Alistair Wood: Another good book to try next. Also begins with three-chord songs.

Ukulele Exercises for Dummies by Brett McQueen and Alistair Wood: Another good book for learning how to practice and improve your ukulele skills. This book is systematic and written by fine teachers.

The Daily Ukulele by Jim and Liz Beloff: This fabulous book is full of good songs – most of the recent tunes are from the 60s and 70s. There is no lesson information, but now that you know five chords you should be able to tackle some of them.

The Daily Ukulele Leap Year Edition by Jim Beloff: More fabulous songs from Jim. This version has more modern tunes by groups such as Black Keys and Green Day.

Easy Songs for Ukulele by Lil' Rev: Fingerpick the melodies of 20 pop, folk, country, and blues songs.

Ukulele Song Books 1 and 2 Many folk and popular songs are written out with words and chords in these two books.

Musicophilia: Tales of Music and the Brain, Revised and Expanded Edition by Oliver Sacks: A scientific exploration of music's physical effect on the human brain. Full of interesting real world stories.

This is Your Brain on Music by Daniel Levitin: Explains our physical and emotional attachment to music, using hundreds of contemporary artists and songs as examples.

About the Authors

Jenny Peters is one part of the sister duo responsible for *21 Songs in 6 Days*. She stumbled upon the ukulele after finding 45 of them in one of her elementary school classrooms. Convinced she could turn her find into more than a whole lot of noise, she designed a program to teach all of her students to play successfully with only 30 minutes of class time a week. No one was more grateful than the teacher in the next classroom.

A former private piano teacher in Chicago with a Masters in Piano Performance from the University of Illinois, Jenny now lives in Highland Park, Illinois. Married with three kids, she shares her home with three cats and more musical instruments than she would care to name.

Rebecca Bogart is the second half of the sister writing team. An acclaimed classical pianist, performer and teacher, Rebecca has been passionate about the piano and music her entire life. She has played for audiences in Italy, taught master classes at Harvard and won more than a few piano competitions. She made her solo debut at Carnegie Hall in early 2014.

Jenny Peters jenny@ukulele.io

Rebecca Bogart rebecca@ukulele.io

facebook.com/21Songsin6Days

Google+ google.com/+Ukuleleio

YouTube ukulele.io/visitYoutube

Twitter @ukuleleio

Made in the USA
San Bernardino, CA
06 October 2016